BENN'S SIXPENNY LIBRARY

ENGLISH FURNITURE

By OLIVER BRACKETT

LONDON: ERNEST BENN LIMITED
BOUVERIE HOUSE, FLEET ST. E.C.

First published 1928

MADE AND PRINTED IN GREAT BRITAIN BY
BILLING AND SONS, LTD., GUILDFORD AND ESHER

EDITORIAL NOTE

THE references to the Great Bed of Ware, Nell Gwyn's Silver Bedstead, and the furnishing of Pepys' house are based on articles by the author, which have already appeared in the *Daily Telegraph*.

CONTENTS

ENGLISH FURNITURE

CHAPTER I

HISTORICAL REVIEW

PART I.—FROM GOTHIC TIMES TO THE COMMONWEALTH
(1400—1660)

IN the social history of a country public attention is
liable to be focussed on the brilliant or tragic careers
of famous men and women, on the magnificence of
their households or the exciting adventures of their
lives. The dirt, disease, and depression which existed
often beneath this romantic exterior is usually over-
looked. Similarly in the study of a nation's furniture
it is a common practice to dwell on the historic or the
magnificent, to select for illustration the exceptional
or sumptuous pieces which were made for distinguished families or great houses. The subject, however, to be properly understood, is one which is closely
interwoven with the lives of the people, depending on
changes in dress, manners and mentality, and reflect-
ing often a variety of foreign influences due to social
or political causes.

It is true that in Gothic times, from about the
thirteenth to the fifteenth centuries, the conditions of
living among the bulk of the people was rude and
primitive, so that, in order to form some conception
of the furniture of the time we have to fall back on
records relating to the houses of the nobles or monastic
establishments. Even then but few actual specimens
of furniture remain, apart from the chests, reading-
desks, stalls, and the like which have survived in

7

churches throughout the country. From such sources much can be learnt of the methods of joinery practised at this time, the nature of the woods in common use, and the character of the decoration generally followed.

Previous to the sixteenth century the country was torn with faction and civil war, so that the castles and houses of the nobles were built rather as fortresses than dwelling houses, and furniture consisted of a few simple types of a movable character which could be transferred from place to place in time of need. The central feature of the house was the great hall, where the family and guests had their meals and lived. Long tables formed of boards and trestles, which could be removed at the end of a meal, were universally found in the hall. Possibly the head of the family had a chair, but the rest of the household sat on forms or stools. Chests, cupboards, and sideboards were also found in the hall, the latter often covered with a cloth for the display of gold or silver plate, to which great importance was attached. Walls were plastered, panelled or hung with tapestry, and the floors usually strewn with rushes. The principal bedchamber also played an important part in the social life of the time.

Most of our knowledge of the life of the period is derived from contemporary literature, inventories and pictorial representations. It is by means of illustrations that scenes of past domestic history can be most vividly imagined, but unfortunately in England there are but few illuminated manuscripts of the Middle Ages which can be studied from this point of view. The Luttrell Psalter in the British Museum, however, contains two scenes of English life in the fourteenth century which are both interesting and instructive. One scene depicts the preparation of a meal, where, at two tables, a cook, wearing a white cap and apron, is chopping meat for his master's table, while men-

BANQUETING SCENE FROM THE LUTTRELL PSALTER, 1340.

servants with shaven upper lips and beards bear the
dishes to the feast in solemn state. The other scene
shows the meal in progress. At a long table formed
of a board and trestles, the latter carved with tracery,
the company is seated side by side against a diaper
background. The host in the centre, an elderly man
wearing a cap with two peaks, has a young woman on
each side, one bareheaded, the other wearing a head-
dress, and among the other guests are two melancholy
monks sitting together. The salt occupies the centre
of the table and a variety of dishes in platters are
depicted. Most of the company are provided with a
knife and spoon, but the food is carried to their
mouths by the fingers, for forks were not yet in use
except for handing fruit or sweetmeats. A servant
arrives bearing two dishes, while in front of the table
a diminutive figure seems to be entertaining the
company by juggling with a circular platter.

There is also in the British Museum an English
illuminated manuscript of a century later (*i.e.*, the
early part of the fifteenth century) depicting a bedroom of the time with wonderful completeness. The
event recorded is the birth of a child. The mother
is shown lying in a sumptuous upholstered bed
with canopy and curtains (but no posts), the material
all covered with a bold diaper pattern and bordered
with fringes. Kneeling at the foot of the bed is an
attendant holding a bowl, while at the side two others
are offering assistance; they wear the tight-waisted
dress of the period and horn-shaped head-dresses. The
room has a stone chimney-piece with an arched opening and three small niches above containing candle-
sticks and reliquaries. Within the hearth a fire of
logs is blazing, supported by two iron fire dogs with
tracery enrichments. In front of the fire a nurse holding a newly-born infant is seated on a chest, the most
typical and useful type of furniture found in bedrooms
of the period. It is somewhat surprising, also, to find

at the side of the bed a chair of peculiar form with rounded back. In the background is a small sideboard covered with a white cloth and supporting silver vessels. The walls appear to be wainscoted with boards or beams painted with sprays of flowers, and the floor is covered with a checker pattern (tiles?) and has a mat in front of the fire. Such records are more effective in bringing the period before our eyes than are isolated examples of furniture, even assuming they could be found. Moreover, they help us to realise how important a part colour played in schemes of decoration in early times, for not only did tapestries, curtains, and cushions contribute to enliven the scene and add to the comfort, but walls and ceilings were vividly painted in primary colours like red, blue, and green, rendered more brilliant by gilding.

*　　　*　　　*　　　*　　　*

The beginning of the sixteenth century in England may be said to have witnessed the death of feudalism and the birth of the Renaissance. The abolition of the monasteries, moreover, brought to an end the autocracy of the church, while the rise of the trading classes introduced a rival element to the power of the nobles. Peace brought security and a more permanent form both in the building and furnishing of houses. The importation of Italian artists at the time of Henry VIII tended to introduce an element of refinement into the native decoration of the country, which was now characterised by the blending of Gothic and Renaissance details of ornament.

Later in the century, in the spacious times of Queen Elizabeth, the spirit of the Renaissance burst out in its fullest splendour. Great changes at this date began to be found in the lives of the people. On such points we have contemporary and reliable evidence in Harrison's *Description of England in the Reign of Elizabeth*. Harrison devoted considerable space to discussing

not only the conditions of living at this period, but made descriptions of the homes and furniture of the people from personal observation. Among other points of interest he drew attention to the fact that the bulk of the buildings in cities and towns were constructed of wood except, to some extent, in the western counties. He made considerable point of the increase in comfort and civilisation which was beginning to affect all classes of society. Manners were becoming more refined, at the table pewter platters and silver spoons were taking the place of the wooden ·implements of an earlier date, the inns throughout the country were both clean and lavishly furnished. With regard to houses and their furniture he wrote:
" The furniture of our houses also excelleth, and is growne in maner even to passing delicacie; and here I do not speake of the nobilitie and gentrie onely, but likewise of the lowest sort in most places of our south countrie, that have anie thing at all to take to. Certes in noble mens houses it is not rare to see abundance of Arras, rich hangings of tapistrie, silver and other vessels, as may furnish sundrie cupboards."
After such reference to the houses of knights, gentlemen, merchantmen and wealthy citizens, he refers to artisans and farmers who " have learned also to garnish their cupboards with plate, their joined beds with tapestry and like hangings and their tables with carpets and fine naperie." The foundation of grammar schools and the spread of learning among the people helped, no doubt, to contribute to this result.

In spite of the changes in social life which seemed so conspicuous to Harrison in his own day, it does not seem, looking back on the times in their true perspective that a striking revolution was taking place, comparable to the social revolution which occurred a century later after the Restoration of Charles II. Rather there resulted, at all events in architecture, decoration, and furniture a gradual development corresponding with some increase in civilisation. In the typical house the great hall still formed the central feature where meals were taken and much of the business of life was conducted, though in the Elizabethan and early Stuart periods, a greater variety of rooms was found, and the Long Gallery, designed for exercise and recreation, made its appearance. The great chamber, which corresponded to the modern drawing-room, was another innovation, and stately wooden staircases began to supplant the spiral stairs of an earlier date.

Walls were panelled with small rectangular panels within framework, but this was only a development of the earliest type of panelling formed of boards placed upright and separated by vertical bars. More importance was attached to colour at the time of Elizabeth and James I. than is commonly supposed, for in addition to brilliant tapestries, hangings, and upholstered furniture, it should be remembered that panelling, chimney-pieces, and ceilings were often painted in bright colours and gilt, so that the somewhat dreary appearance of furnished interiors of this period, as seen to-day with colour removed and materials faded, gives an entirely false impression of the original effect.

The furniture of the Elizabethan and early Stuart periods showed a gradual development parallel to contemporary architecture without altering in general character. Broadly speaking, it still belonged to the heavy type made usually of oak, though in the case of important pieces, walnut was not infrequently found. Heavy carving was characteristic of the period, as well as inlay in woods from native trees like apple, pear, and holly. A few conspicuous developments should be noticed. The chair began to take its place as a comparatively common article of domestic utility, although during the Elizabethan period joined stools and forms were still in general use. No longer did circumstances demand movable tables formed of boards and trestles, and by the first half of the seventeenth century they are found commonly of solid form, sometimes of great length (refectory tables), but gradually becoming smaller and in other cases capable of being lengthened by two wings (draw tables) ingeniously fitted into the framework. Chests still formed a necessary part of house furniture, but from the chest developed other types, of which the court cupboard is a conspicuous example. Boxes and desks were now used for the disposal of small articles of clothing or trinkets of value. The sideboard formed of two shelves placed one above the other was a direct descendant of the medieval sideboard, though now elaborated with carving and inlay and a variety of mouldings. Although the bedroom had less importance as a centre of social life than previously, the bedstead continued to hold its place as the most respected piece of furniture in the house. In farmhouses similar furniture of solid and primitive character was found in addition to hutches, bread cupboards, corn bins, high-back settles, and other types which the particular functions of country life demanded.

How few were the types of furniture in use even in the great houses, yet how rich in colour and romance can be gathered from the description of a bedroom taken from the " Inventory of the Castle of Arundel " made in the reign of Elizabeth :

"*The Square Chamber*. Item, iii pieces of hangings of okes and white horses. Item, i bedsteede of wallnut-tree, with tester of crymson velvett imbroidered wth. cloth of golde, and V crymson silk curtains wth. one counterpoynt of crymson taffeta lined with white fustia, to the same. One chier and two long cusshions of the same stuffe to the same bedd. Item, i fetherbedd and boulster, i pillowe, iii rugges and ii fustia

blancketts thereto. Item, i pallet bedd uppo the
floore, i boulster, i covering of verders and one
pallet-case of canvas. Item, one old cubberd of
waynescotte. Item, one carpett of greene cloth for
the cubberd. Item, i paier of andirons of iron."

Most of the rooms in important houses of the
period were hung with tapestry, while Turkey carpets
were found on the floors and sometimes placed on
tables and cupboards. Crimson velvet was a popular
material for curtains and cushions, though blue and
green in various materials were favoured colours.
Thus with chimney-pieces and ceilings partly painted
and gilt, and silver vessels displayed on the sideboard, an effect of almost theatrical brilliance must
have been often obtained.

There is but little to be said of English furniture
during the Commonwealth. The wonderful contents
of the royal palaces, both in London and the country,
consisting of paintings, furniture, and gold and silver
plate were sold by auction with the exception of
various tapestries which were retained for the use of
the Protector. Many of the paintings were recovered
after the Restoration, but a vast wealth of artistic
treasures was thus irrevocably lost to the nation.

PART II.—FROM THE RESTORATION TO THE
NINETEENTH CENTURY

(1660—1800)

THE Restoration of the Monarchy in 1660 marks a
break in the chain of evolution, to which there is no
other parallel in English history. It witnessed, in fact,
a complete revolution in social life, a breaking with the
past in mentality, manners, dress, building, decoration
and furniture. As far as the arts are concerned, this
was something quite unlike the changes in fashion

which have from time to time occurred. The Gothic,
Chinese, and Etruscan cults, for instance, in the
eighteenth century, were but ripples on the surface of
the steady stream of development, and had nothing in
common with the violent reaction against tradition,
which coincided with the return of Charles II.

It was not unnatural that after the depression of the
Commonwealth the pendulum should swing rapidly in
the opposite direction. The example set by a brilliant
and licentious court was eagerly followed by a people
whose spirits had been dulled by years of apathy. The
expensive mistresses of Charles II. vied with one
another in the luxury of their households, and the
best families in the land lived up to the new traditions.
A great stimulus was given to building, decoration,
and furnishing, and entertainment was conducted on
a scale of magnificence which is difficult to realize in
modern days of economy. John Evelyn has left a
striking description of a house-party at Euston, the
country seat of Lord Arlington, given in honour of
Charles II. for Newmarket Races. "Came all the
great men," he wrote, "from Newmarket and other
parts both of Suffolk and Norfolk, to make their court,
the whole house filled from one end to the other with
lords, ladies, and gallants; there was such a furnished
table, as I had seldom seen, nor anything more
splendid and free, so that for fifteen days there were
entertained at least 200 people, and half as many
horses, besides servants and guards, at infinite
expense." He described how the days were passed
with hunting and hawking, followed by cards and
dice till almost morning.

It may be said, in a sense, that this period of English
history marks the end of antiquarianism and the beginning of modernity. The typical house which had
developed from the medieval castle gave way before
the Italian plan adopted by Sir Christopher Wren and
his contemporaries. Starting from the hall and leading

one from the other would be usually found a succession of rooms designed to satisfy the varied needs of civilization, the dining-room, salon, library, office, while upper floors were devoted to bedrooms. All details of proportion were systematically calculated; light penetrated through tall, sash windows; long, restful panels lined the walls. The citizen's house of the time, with passage and staircase, dining-room on ground floor, parlour and bedrooms above, an arrangement generally followed throughout the eighteenth century, differs little in essentials from the modern middle-class dwelling-house.

In a similar spirit the furniture of the latter part of the seventeenth century cast off the heavy cloak of tradition and clad itself in lighter and more fantastic garb. The solid tables and buffets of Elizabeth were unsuited to the new style with its fastidious and foreign affectations. New types of furniture were necessary, new woods, new methods of decoration. Chairs and day-beds with spiral turning and cane seats and backs of French or Flemish character supplanted the solid framed chairs of a previous generation. Cabinets with small drawers became all the rage, and the cabinet-maker came on the scene for the first time. From the cabinet sprang the bureau-bookcase and other types. The collecting of books was becoming fashionable, and bookcases with glass doors were in demand—for the introduction of glass was a distinguishing feature in the new taste. The primitive chest was passing out of fashion, but mounted on a stand and fitted with drawers developed into the chest of drawers, a type which has passed through the eighteenth century to modern times practically unaltered. Long case and bracket clocks, tripod candlestands, small tables both square and circular, mirrors and sconces formed part of the furnishing of typical rooms. Bedsteads crowned with plumes and hung with rich silks and velvets introduced another alien element, though producing a brilliant effect in unison with the upholstered chairs and love seats which the new luxury demanded.

Oak, essentially English and suitable to the panelled rooms of an earlier age, had previously been the wood in common use, but the new taste for foreign fashions brought walnut wood into general favour. Walnut, with its fine grain and surface capable of brilliant polish, was, moreover, eminently suited to the lighter and more fastidious types of furniture which began now to appeal to the public. But whether through reasons of expense or because the demand was greater than the supply, the process of " veneering " or the overlay of woods of fine quality on a plain carcase began to be generally adopted. Thus considerable scope for ornamental effect was obtained by the selection of woods of varied and often vivid marking. Work of this type was sometimes arranged in the form of patterns in marquetry of woods of varying colour and texture, with designs in which human figures, birds, butterflies, flowers, and scrolls were represented.

Another process of decoration which became fashionable after about 1660 was lacquer work or " japanning," the taste for this work lasting throughout the eighteenth century. In furniture ornamented in this manner panels were sometimes sent out to the East to be lacquered, and afterwards made up in England; in other cases the lacquer work was done at home in the Oriental style. Japanning became a fashionable amusement for ladies—hence the amateurish character of much of the work which, partly for sentimental reasons, is now so highly prized. Much of this so-called English lacquer is, in reality, merely paint. Cabinets, tables, clocks, chairs, dressing-glasses, and mirror-frames were covered with designs of Oriental character, the ornament being gilded on black or blue, and more rarely on a red, yellow, or tortoiseshell ground.

The height of luxury was reached at this date by silver furniture, which took the form of tables, mirrors, and candelabra, as well as caskets and articles for the toilet such as were used by ladies. As a rule, furniture of this type had a wooden basis carved with floral ornament and armorial devices, over which were laid thin plates of beaten silver. It was, of course, only in the royal households or the great houses that this extravagant work was found. Evelyn, moralizing on the vices of the age, referred to "great vases of wrought plate, tables, stands, chimney furniture, sconces, branches, braseras, etc., all of massy silver and out of number" in the apartments at Whitehall Palace of Louise de Kerouaille, afterwards Duchess of Portsmouth, the French mistress of Charles II.

It is a far cry from such pomps and vanities to the dreary and uneventful lives of the middle classes. How far did the common people catch the echo of the prevailing fashions? In London, to a small extent, we can imagine, but hardly at all in the country. The Great Fire swept away a large proportion of the old wooden houses in the City and whatever primitive furniture they may have contained. This was an opportunity for rebuilding as well as furnishing in the modern style, but most of the simple furniture of this type, being too artistically unimportant to preserve, has not survived the vicissitudes of two and a half centuries. Changes of taste and novelties of fashion filtered but slowly into country districts and traditional forms of the early Stuart period lingered on well past the Restoration and sometimes into the eighteenth century. The homes of prosperous farmers and the smaller manor houses were still for many years furnished (as dated examples of the end of the seventeenth and beginning of the eighteenth century attest) with heavy oak cupboards, solid chests, chairs, and tables differing only in minor details from pieces made at the time of James I.

It is possible to form some idea of the character of the middle-class homes at this period from the pages of the diary of Samuel Pepys. There is perhaps no record in the English language in which the truth stands revealed in such stark nakedness as in these " Jekyll-and-Hyde " confessions. Pepys was a hard worker, but he managed to allow himself considerable relaxation— to visit the play, engage in amorous adventures with " my little she milliner," and many others, and hold converse with all sorts and conditions of men. To the furniture of his house, moreover, he devoted much attention.

In 1660, on his appointment to the post of " Clerk to the King's Ships," Pepys, with his wife, moved to a residence attached to the Navy Office between Crutched Friars and Seething Lane. The house must have been in a bad state of repair, for during the first year or two workmen were engaged in structural alterations, reflooring the rooms, putting in new doors, and repainting throughout the house. Almost every morning Pepys was found "among my workmen," and sometimes he gave the whole day to them with not a little fretfulness when progress was delayed. The principal rooms were redecorated, and in October, 1660, it was noted : " This morning my dining-room was finished with green serge hanging and gilt leather, which is very handsome." In the following year the entrance hall was enlarged and a new staircase put up. Probably the panelling of the dining-room consisted of long panels with a chair rail, such as became universal (though first introduced in a small way by Inigo Jones at the time of Charles I.) in buildings of the school of Sir Christopher Wren. The long panels would be covered with the gilt leather to which reference has been made, and the serge hangings served, no doubt, as curtains to the windows. Panelled rooms with leather-covered hangings were not uncommon at this period, though in most cases the leather has since perished or been taken down. The staircase, no doubt, belonged to the new type, with spiral or column balusters, for the heavy newel posts of the time of Elizabeth were no longer fashionable. There is a note to show that in 1661 the chimney-pieces and pictures in the dining-room were gilt. A few years afterwards the decoration of the dining-room was evidently completed with painted panels probably over the chimney-piece and doors, for we read : " This afternoon I called with my wife at Dancre's, the great landscape painter, by Mr. Povy's advice; and have bespoke him to take measure of my dining-room panels . . ." (and a short time afterwards): "And he took measure of my panels in my dining-room, where, in the four, I intend to have the four houses of the King, White Hall, Hampton Court, Greenwich, and Windsor."

From time to time Pepys added to the furniture of his house, buying in 1661 for his own room a chest of drawers (a type of furniture only just coming into use), as well as a pair of candlestands and a hanging shelf for his wife's chamber. A spinet by Hayward was another acquisition. The house in the end must have been furnished in good style and taste, for in 1667 there is a note " doing some things to my house, which will cost money—that is, furnish our best chamber with tapestry and other rooms with pictures." The bedrooms were furnished with hangings of different colours, in one case red, and in another case green, and had Turkey-work chairs.

*   *   *   *   *

Although the eighteenth century in England witnessed a gradual development in architecture, decoration and furniture, the broad stream of progress was constantly interrupted by a variety of conflicting cross-currents. Fortunes were made by speculation and the *nouveaux riches* vied with the aristocracy in building houses of ambitious architectural character, decorated and furnished in the style of magnificence characteristic of the period, fitted often with a library of the world's great literature and embellished with masterpieces of painting and sculpture collected on their travels abroad. Italy was crowded with English travellers who, if they were not popular in themselves, were at least popular in the lavish way they spent their money. Palladio was adopted as an architectural model and mansions based on Italian villas were erected throughout the country irrespective of considerations of climate. To the Englishman the eighteenth century was an age of restlessness, experiment, curiosity, and affectation. A writer in a paper called the *Lounger* summed up the position in 1786 with caustic truthfulness : " A well-educated British gentleman, it may be truly said, is of no country whatever, he unites in himself the characteristics of all different nations; he talks and dresses French, and sings Italian; he rivals the Spaniard in indolence, and the German in drinking, his house is Grecian, his offices Gothic, and his furniture Chinese."

It was a snobbish age, moreover, when titles were worshipped with blind idolatry, and authors and artists dedicated their works to noble patrons in high-flown language of cringing servility. Sharply defined also were the divisions separating one class of society from another. Thus it came about that in building and furnishing a distinct style, a style of pompous magnificence, runs all through the eighteenth century in the houses of the wealthy while the middle classes were following another and simpler tradition. This is particularly noticeable during the reigns of the first three Georges, for the furniture of the period of Queen Anne in general character differed but little from the work of the time of the late Stuarts and William III., to which we have already referred. The typical Queen Anne chair, of Dutch origin, with solid vase-shaped splat and cabriole legs and claw-and-ball foot was an innovation, and one which lasted for many years. But the bureau-bookcases, card-tables, tea-tables, tall case clocks, sconces, and candlestands, first brought into fashion in the latter part of the seventeenth century, merely developed with slight alterations during the reign of Queen Anne. The period of the first two Georges, however, produced in the great houses a peculiar type of gilt furniture of Venetian character, with which the name of William Kent is associated. This work consisted of heavy side-tables, writing-tables, candelabra, mirrors, and pedestals, carved with human masks and scrolls, and all intended to occupy a definite place in the Palladian rooms, for which they were designed. They were usually covered with gilding, but sometimes made of mahogany (which was just coming into fashion) and partly gilt. This tradition was carried on later in the century by Robert Adam, who made numbers of designs for commodes, couches, chairs, sideboards, pedestals, wine-coolers, carpets, and the like, the quality of the work being refined under the Roman, Pompeian, and other influences which affected this school of architecture. In decoration carving began to give way before inlay and painting.

Now, neither Kent nor Adam had any sympathy whatever with the middle classes and the furnishing of their unromantic homes, nor were the highly ornate designs of these fashionable architects suitable to the house of the average man. The bulk of the people, with which we include prosperous men of business and the professional classes, required comparatively simple furniture to satisfy the needs of everyday life, though they may have found a natural pleasure in decoration to a reasonable extent and to the limit of their purses. There is one source of information which gathers up the tangled threads of this question and straightens them out for our understanding in Chippendale's *Gentleman and Cabinet-Maker's Director,* which was published just after the middle of the eighteenth century.

The career and character of this historically famous cabinet-maker cannot be properly considered in a few lines, and we propose to discuss him in a separate chapter; but the value of his book in relation to the points we are considering lies in the fact that he tried to appeal in his designs to the average man who desired simplicity as well as to the prosperous and wealthy patron who required magnificence at any cost. His book illustrates every type of furniture which was in use in England by the middle of the eighteenth century, in addition to a certain number of fantastic compositions which were imaginative essays rather than practical models. His designs include chairs, sofas, bedsteads, window-cornices, bed-cornices, china tables, dressing-tables, breakfast-tables, shaving-tables, basin-stands, tea-kettle-stands, sideboards, commodes, writing-tables, bookcases, organs, combined desks and bookcases, chests of drawers, toilet-tables, cabinets, clothes-chests, china cases, hanging shelves, candle-stands, pedestals, cisterns, lanterns, chandeliers, fire-screens, tea-caddies, brackets, clock cases, mirror frames, console tables, girandoles, picture-frames, and stove grates. Although in these designs Chippendale borrowed from every available source, he was largely dependent for inspiration on the French rococo, though he flirted to a considerable extent with the Chinese and Gothic fashions, which had short vogues of popularity in the mid-eighteenth century.

A large proportion of these pieces of furniture had been in use since the time of Charles II., but a certain number of new types of a domestic nature were introduced, showing that there was growing up a tendency to more fastidiousness in the personal habits of daily life. This is noticeable in the case of the bedroom. Until the middle of the eighteenth century the furniture of the bedroom, as inventories attest, consisted almost always of a bedstead, a table (probably used as a dressing-table), a pair of candlestands, a wardrobe or chest, and perhaps a chair or stool. Occasionally a basin might be mentioned, but no references are made to washstands, and probably Chippendale's designs for basin-stands are the earliest known examples of this type of furniture. There is, however, plenty of evidence to show that washing of the face, hands, and body was practised in England as far back as the Middle Ages, though the practice was not treated with the same seriousness as habit or fashion demands at the present day. But, apart from sentiment, there was probably a more practical reason in the difficulty of obtaining an unlimited supply of water. It is true that after the sixteenth century London was supplied with water by means of wooden pipes, but the average householder had probably to fetch his water from a pump or well. This water scarcity was probably the cause of the small size of the basins and bottles in use in the eighteenth century.

Chippendale's designs for basin-stands are pretty good evidence that the washstand was coming into fashion, and undoubtedly genuine examples of this type of furniture exist at the present day. Some twenty years later the firm of Hepplewhite published a few designs, which seem to have been unintelligently adopted from Chippendale. It is not till the end of the century that a marked development was found. Sheraton, who was apparently among the first to use the term " wash-hand stand," showed considerable ingenuity in this type of furniture. By the end of the century, in fact, the washstand had become a common article of furniture, and was often distinguished for the elaboration of its fittings.

That the English in the seventeenth and eighteenth centuries were not distinguished for cleanliness seems fairly certain, but it is probable that they did not differ in this respect from the other nations of Europe. It has been suggested that in the eighteenth century ladies of fashion avoided the irksomeness of washing their faces by the use of paint, laying one coat over another. On the other hand, the practice of painting the face was not generally favoured in England. Etheredge, in the *Man of Mode,* written in 1676, had something to say of "Young ladies who notoriously wash and paint, though they have naturally good complexions." And Lady Mary Wortley Montagu, who lived for the most part on the Continent, remarked that English women abroad could be distinguished by the naturalness of their complexions.

Intimate memoirs of the seventeenth and eighteenth centuries have occasional references to the subject of washing, but more particularly to the bath. Even the great town and country houses had no bathrooms, though baths were usually found in the Royal Palaces. At Hampton Court there is a peculiar alcove-shaped marble bath in one of the bedrooms, and in Hamilton's *Mémoires du Comte de Gramont* an incident in the baths of one of the Royal Palaces is discussed at some length. Among the middle classes the bath was a very unusual event. Pepys devoted a day or two of his diary to his experience of this sensation. Casanova, travelling in England in 1763, surprised the elusive Miss Charpillon in the bath—the young woman on whose account he afterwards set out with stones in his pocket to commit suicide in the Thames.

*   *   *   *   *

The last quarter of the eighteenth century showed a change in mentality in the English people. The stilted and pedantic mannerisms which had characterized both art and literature, the ponderous and measured literary style, the deadly accurate but soulless Palladian building, began to give way before the craving for more natural expression and greater freedom of thought in different fields of human endeavour. The echo of the rumbling storm heralding the revolution in France could be faintly heard on this side of the

Channel. The thoughts of the people began to be occupied with the cult of liberty and the rights of man. The circulation of newspapers was tending to spread intelligence through all ranks of society.

The classical revival in architecture associated with the name of Robert Adam sounded the death-knell of the Palladian fashion as well as the rococo, Chinese, and Gothic crazes which had brief periods of popularity in the middle of the eighteenth century. The style of architecture evolved by Adam and adopted by his contemporaries has been classified and analysed in great detail. Everyone is familiar with the typical Adam house, cold and severe, yet relieved often by brilliantly executed decoration enriched with colour and gilding. Panelling in wood was no longer demanded, for the new style favoured blank walls relieved often with medallions of classical figures in plaster, and friezes in which rams' head, Greek honeysuckle, and foliage executed with extreme delicacy vere favourite motives of decoration. These refined nd sensitive schemes of ornament required furniture similar character. Robert Adam, who regarded the nishing of the house as part of the architectural eption, himself made designs for a variety of types rniture. To a certain extent his designs may be ered original, though he obtained inspiration i arious sources, from Roman ornament, from the It Renaissance, and the French style of Louis XVI. M f his work deserves to rank with historic exa of the world's furniture. Such is the " Diana and rva " commode at Harewood, executed by Chip le from Adam's design in 1773, and descri s follows in the accounts :

ery large rich commode with exceeding fin ique Ornaments curiously inlaid with vari ne woods, Drawers at each end and enclo vith folding Doors, with Diana and

Minerva and their emblems curiously inlaid and
engraved, a Cupboard in the middle part with a
Coved Door, a Dressing Drawer in the Top part,
the whole Elegantly Executed and varnished, with
many wrought Brass Antique Ornaments finely
finished.   £86 os. od."

In their designs most of the cabinet-makers of the
day followed in the footsteps of Robert Adam, though
their work was of a simpler character and more suited
to the tastes of the middle classes. There is the case of
George Hepplewhite, a cabinet-maker who served an
apprenticeship with the firm of Gillow, and afterwards
opened a shop in Cripplegate. On his death in 1786
the business was carried on by his widow, Alice
Hepplewhite, in whose name a book of designs
entitled *The Cabinet-maker's and Upholsterer's Guide*
was published. Nothing much seems to be known
about the merits of the Hepplewhites as craftsmen, but
their book is useful as showing the evolution of furniture design in England towards the end of the
eighteenth century. Taste was constantly changing,
and it is amusing to note how each new author
expressed a tolerant approval of the last, though
admitting his designs to be already out of date. At the
end of the eighteenth and beginning of the nineteenth
century another author, Thomas Sheraton, devoted a
vast amount of labour to putting on record the
character of contemporary furniture in the form of
published books. Sheraton, however, was mainly a
theorist, and should not be ranked with the practical
cabinet-makers of his day. Among the latter the firms
of Seddon and Gillow held a high place. According to
the *Annual Register* for 1768, " A dreadful fire burnt
down London House, formerly the residence of the
Bishops of London, now occupied by Mr. Seddon, one
of the most eminent Cabinet-makers in London." This
was probably Thomas Seddon, who came from Man-

chester and founded the firm. His son continued in
the business, which was known as Seddon Sons and
Shackleton, and had premises in Aldersgate. The
Gillows were also a Lancashire firm, and had been
associated with the town of Lancaster since the time
of William and Mary. In the second half of the
eighteenth century they appear to have opened a
branch in London, and the name is found associated
with this type of business to the present day.

The French Revolution and the war with France
put a check on the development of all the arts in
England. Economy and simplicity became the fashion.
Building and furnishing made no progress. An echo
of the Empire style, without its symbolism, was found
in English decoration. Imperial eagles and purple
curtains became popular. Then the Egyptian fashion
had a short vogue of popularity. It was, in a sense, a
pathetic period of history, full of unsettled ambitions
when traditions were falling away, and there seemed
nothing to take their place. In a later chapter we have
discussed the tendencies of these days as well as the
character of the Victorian period, which followed.

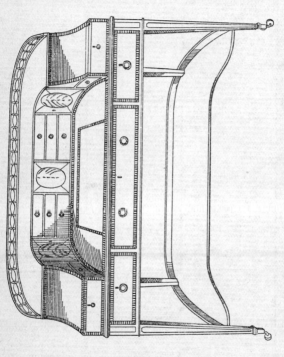

DRAWING AND WRITING TABLE. SHERATON, 1791.

CHAPTER II

THE DECORATION OF ROOMS

THERE are many reasons why furniture is interesting to the people. There are those who regard the subject from the collector's point of view, and aim at acquiring the most valuable and ornamental examples of various periods. Others have a critical interest in methods of construction or processes of decoration. A certain school, further, studies the subject in its relation to the domestic history of a country. But in the main the subject appeals to the public because people have homes of their own, and in the furnishing of them find inspiration in the decorative schemes of the past. A well-known writer in a Sunday paper recently discussing modern tendencies, has prophesied that in the future the home will only be used as a place in which to sleep, but at present we have not arrived at this advanced or retrograde stage of civilisation.

Although a piece of furniture regarded as an individual specimen may be interesting or attractive historically or technically, the subject of furnishing to be properly understood must, in a broad sense, be considered in relation to the house and its fittings. In England panelled walls, painted plaster-work, tapestries, damask hangings, or wall-papers have provided the backgrounds against which oak, walnut, mahogany, or satinwood furniture have at different periods been placed. Panelling and hangings had originally a utilitarian purpose, being intended to serve as preventive against cold, but as human nature always craves for colour and ornament, they are found even from early times enriched with ornament, at first

35

crudely, and later more elaborately as civilisation advanced.

The earliest form of panelling, consisting of boards placed upright and separated by vertical bars, had given way by the early Tudor period to a definite type of panelling which in essentials lasted till the time of Charles II. This consisted of rectangular panels, usually of oak framed by upright rails joined by vertical stiles fixed by mortise and tenons. The edges of the upright rails were generally cut with a rounded moulding, and the upper edge of the stiles were bevelled. Later on, by the time of Elizabeth, this primitive method of treatment had given way to the practice of attaching mouldings of some elaboration above, below, and at each side of the panel. As to the further ornamentation of this type of panelling, no definite laws can be laid down, for according to circumstances it might be left plain or covered with carving, often painted and gilt. At the time of Henry VIII. panels were often carved either with linenfold ornament or heads within medallions or heraldic shields, but rails or stiles were not ornamented.

The most ornamental feature of the room during the Tudor and early Stuart period was the chimneypiece. This was the central feature of the composition and was usually carved in high relief. Frequently the chimney-piece bore in the middle the coat-of-arms of the family to whom the house belonged, and the Royal Arms were often found, though introduced sometimes more from reasons of loyalty than any other. Ceilings were commonly of plaster, often covered with designs in which floral ornament or sometimes figure designs were arranged within panels formed of intersecting bands. It often happened that both panelling and ceilings were painted in bright colours and gilded. Sometimes the panels were ornamented with stencilled arabesques. More often than

CHIMNEY-PIECE AT BLICKLING HALL, NORFOLK, 1627.

HNRY VIII

not this painted decoration has been destroyed at later dates, but examples can still be found in an untouched condition.

The revolution in taste after the restoration of the monarchy in 1660 had a marked effect on the fitting and decoration of rooms. The traditional form of panelling with small rectangular panels and heavy chimney-piece was superseded by a new type based in proportions on the classical orders of architecture. Walls were covered with long, rectangular panels stretching from cornice to dado rail, the latter running round all sides of the room and broken only by the chimney-piece and doors; the panels projected beyond the surface of the wall and were framed by mouldings. Windows were of the same shape as the long panels and were fitted with glazed sashes having small rectangular panes—a fashion which, originally derived from Holland, has continued in favour in England to modern times. Chimney-pieces usually had a marble moulding of bolection section surrounding the opening of the fireplace. On the overmantel would be found a rectangular panel containing a painting, sometimes a portrait, at other times a landscape or pastoral scene; similar paintings were often placed over the doors. Occasionally a long mirror would be inset into the overmantel. The character of wood-carving underwent great changes at this date. Festoons of flowers, fruit, and leaves in the realistic manner of Grinling Gibbons were favoured as frames to paintings on overmantels or walls. Cornices and frames of doors were commonly carved with classical acanthus foliage.

There was a certain severity about the panelled rooms of the latter part of the seventeenth century, a period associated with the name of Sir Christopher Wren. The woods in popular use were either walnut or oak, both of which are capable of a fine quality of surface. It is not surprising, therefore, to find that the panelled rooms of this date were left, as a rule, in the natural wood. In rare cases the panels were covered with pictorial representations, and were sometimes hung with tapestry or damask. In keeping with the unpainted walls were the plaster ceilings, sometimes ornamented in high relief with wreaths of flowers and leaves after the realistic manner of Grinling Gibbons. But severe as were the decorative schemes of the late Stuart period, the general effect of the rooms was by no means dull. In some of the great houses and palaces ceilings were painted with classical and allegorical figure subjects by Verrio, Laguerre, and other fashionable artists who had been imported from abroad. Brilliant in the extreme also were the fabrics used as curtains for the windows and coverings for the settees and chairs. Figured velvets and damasks of many colours—crimson, blue, or yellow—adorned with fringes must have produced a vivid effect in conjunction with the walnut, lacquered, and marquetry furniture which was finding its way into popular favour.

During the first half of the eighteenth century the architects of the day were obsessed with the principles of Palladianism, and this outlook was reflected in contemporary interior decoration. A slavish worship of the Orders of Architecture produced a style which sacrificed everything to correctness of proportions based on mathematical calculation. A certain soullessness resulted. These qualities are found in typical rooms of the early Georgian period, where the centre is occupied by a chimney-piece with overmantel in one piece, and doors and windows are placed exactly to balance one another. In carved decoration typical features of ornament were blank shields, human masks, pendants of foliage, and Greek scroll borders. Apart from changes of style, the panelled rooms of this date can be distinguished from those of the late Stuart period in the fact that pinewood had succeeded oak and walnut as the wood in common use. But as

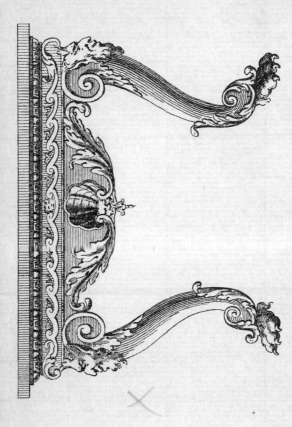

DESIGN FOR SIDE TABLE. WILLIAM JONES, 1739.

2*

pine has an undistinguished appearance, it became the common practice to paint the surface white, blue, green, or brown, and often to gild the carvings. An effect of considerable richness was thus obtained which agreed with the somewhat heavy mahogany furniture now in fashion.

It was during the eighteenth century that wall-papers came into general use in England. Late in the seventeenth century it seems to have been realized that the effect of figured velvet could be obtained at a low cost by paper. A considerable demand arose, therefore, for papers or wall-hangings reproducing the bold diaper patterns found on Italian velvets and brocades. That there was a recognized trade in such papers is shown by a reference in the *London Gazette* for 1693. "At the Warehouse for New fashion'd Hangings . . . are made and sold strong Paper-Hangings . . . at Three-pence per yard." They were printed from small blocks and sprinkled with flock in order to produce a velvety appearance. Of these flock papers a certain number have been preserved in country houses— as at Christchurch Mansion, near Ipswich—and are re-markably attractive in general effect.

The Chinese vogue in the eighteenth century was responsible, among other things, for Chinese wall-papers. These were usually painted by hand with flowering trees and birds in vivid colours. Brilliant as these wall-papers often were, they were apparently not considered to be of great importance, and were usually put up in bedrooms as a background to lacquered furniture. At Nostell Priory in Yorkshire one of these papers was hung by Chippendale, who evidently made the green lacquered bedstead and wardrobe in the same room. Another fashion in wall-papers at this date is associated with the name of Jackson of Battersea, who claimed to have invented a process of printing from wood blocks in ten positive tints, with the use of oil colour to obtain permanency. In 1754 Jackson published a book explaining his method of printing, which, he declared, "exceeds every other hitherto known," and expressed contempt for the contemporary Chinese papers. Some idea of his work can be obtained from one of Horace Walpole's letters describing his villa at Strawberry Hill:

> "Now you shall walk into the house; the low window leads into a little parlour hung with a stone-coloured Gothic paper and Jackson's Venetian prints; from hence you come to the hall and staircase; imagine the walls covered with (I call it paper in perspective to represent) Gothic fretwork. . . . The room on the ground floor nearest you is a bed-chamber hung with yellow paper and prints framed in a manner invented by Lord Cadogan, with black and white borders printed."

One room had a green paper and water-colour pictures, another a blue and white paper adorned with festoons, while the walls of a third were covered with paper imitating Dutch tiles.

CHAPTER III

THE EVOLUTION OF TYPES

IT is an interesting matter to follow the evolution of the most obvious types of furniture and note the causes which influenced their development. Manners becoming more and more fastidious as civilization advanced played an important part in altering the character of types of furniture. But changes of fashion, sometimes merely temporary, have to be considered as well as eccentricities in dress and foreign influences.

We have already explained that up to the early Stuart period the chair was not an item of furnishing in common use. Most of the earliest chairs were solid box-like structures, fitted with arms and often carved with linenfold ornament or tracery. By the time of Elizabeth, though still of heavy build, the chair is found fitted with legs joined by stretchers. They were not constructed in a way to lend themselves to comfort, though their harshness could be relieved by loose cushions, sometimes of leather and at other times of velvet and other materials. By the middle of the seventeenth century upholstery was applied to the framework, but the form known later as an " easy chair " had not yet appeared. A peculiar and rare type in the sixteenth century, copied from an Italian model, had a semi-circular back, and was covered with upholstery; such is the well-known chair at Moreton-in-Marsh, on which Charles I. is supposed to have sat during his trial.

The first great change came at the time of Charles II. when, following the new craze for foreign elegance, a French or Flemish model was adopted, with cane seat and back within framework of scrolls and scrolled legs joined by stretchers. These chairs were commonly made of walnut, but sometimes of beech, and were often carved with cherubs, coronets and leafage. Comfort was not much considered in their design, nor are they much to be commended for strength or durability. On the other hand, winged armchairs heavily padded and covered with velvets, damasks or embroidery now came into fashion, suggesting a greater ease and luxury than was known in earlier days. Towards the end of the seventeenth century chairs became cramped and narrow with tall backs, often approaching absurdity; the scroll was abandoned and cup-shaped legs and curved stretchers were common features.

The reign of Queen Anne saw the introduction of a new type, owing its origin to Dutch influence. This new form of chair had a rounded back, solid vase-shaped splat, carved legs and claw-and-ball feet. It was an excellent model, strong, yet shapely, and usually intelligently ornamented with carved shells on the knees or inlay of flowers on the back. Chippendale and his contemporaries borrowed and elaborated this model, piercing the splat and substituting (as a rule) straight legs and stretchers. It cannot be said, however, that the chairs of this period showed any advance in design. The prevalent passion for display led the chair-makers of the day to commit frequent errors of judgment. Such is the case of the ribbon-back chair, for which Chippendale expressed great admiration, where the splat is most unsuitably carved in open-work with fluttering ribbons.

Towards the end of the century Robert Adam evolved a type of chair which is strongly to be commended for its sound sense and elegant proportions. This type, which was based on a French model of the time of Louis XVI., had a solid oval back covered with upholstery, and a gilt framework, with fluted tapering legs. The chair-makers of 1780 and thereabouts seem to have gone further in solving the problem of the chair than any of their predecessors by adopting the policy of elegance combined with utility, and using ornament with caution and judgment. The oval back was generally adopted at this date and competed for popularity with the shield form, but gave way to the square back towards the end of the century. Chairs made in the nineteenth century had no particular qualities to which special attention need be drawn.

The position of the table is even more consistently interwoven with domestic history than that of the chair, for the table has been a common article of furniture from medieval times. The earliest form, the board and trestle, is a natural product of a restless and uncertain age. A more settled state of society produced solid tables, but various devices have always existed for making the table adaptable to different purposes. An exception is the so-called "refectory" table, found in Tudor and early Stuart times, consisting of a long, narrow board supported on legs joined by stretchers and intended to be placed permanently against the long seats of a hall. But even in the sixteenth century the problem of lengthening a table was tackled, and resulted in the invention of the "draw table," with two wings on runners which could be pulled out from beneath the top. This model gave way in popularity to the type commonly known as the "gate-leg" table, in which two open frames or gates fitting into a central framework could be pulled out to support hinged flaps. This table remained in general use until well into the eighteenth century, and although a clumsy and uneasy model, still retains its popularity at the present day. After the Restoration, dining-tables assumed this form, and large parties were obliged to dine at separate tables. The tendency from this date leant in general towards lighter furniture, and circular tables with pillar and tripod-stand came into fashion, and were used during the eighteenth century for the service of tea and many other purposes. Other fashions produced new types. The passion for gambling brought into general use the card-table with hinged top, a type which, for its particular purpose, has never been improved upon. About the middle of the eighteenth century the " Pembroke " table with hinged flaps, supported on brackets fitting into the framework, came to be recognized as probably the most simple and convenient type of table which common sense could devise. It was not, however, adapted for bearing heavy weights nor suitable for dining purposes. For the latter, long solid tables came into use, built in such a way that their length could be increased by the insertion of leaves in the centre. A few peculiar types were born and died in the eighteenth century. Such is the " china table " with fretwork rim and pierced legs, a ridiculous model by reason of its excessive fragility. If the question is considered without prejudice, it must be admitted that the table is not a type of furniture which lends itself to decoration. It is reasonable enough in certain circumstances to ornament the frieze below the top or carve the knees or feet, but to cover the top with elaborate decoration in marquetry, lacquer or gesso—as was done often with great skill in the late Stuart period—is a case of throwing to the winds the elementary law of suitability of purpose.

There are types of furniture which are essential to domestic life at any time, while others rather owe their origin to the manners or habits of a particular date. The sideboard, though in character it has undergone great changes, is found all through English history from Gothic times to the present day, and the wardrobe has had a similar development. But the chest, which was the commonest and most useful piece of furniture in early times, had gone out of fashion by the eighteenth century, when society was becoming more complex. Other types had even shorter lives. The tall candlestand, which at the time of Charles II. was

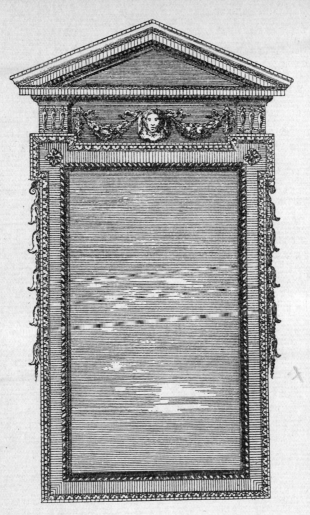

DESIGN FOR MIRROR FRAME.   WILLIAM JONES, 1739.

universally found in the bedrooms of persons of any position, did not survive to any extent beyond the eighteenth century. The long case clock had a similar career, though the bracket clock has lasted to modern times.

Putting aside the primitive devices of the Middle Ages, the history of the mirror does not go back farther than the time when looking-glass plates were first made in England. In the early part of the seventeenth century Sir Robert Mansell obtained the services of " many expert strangers from foreign parts beyond the seas to instruct the natives of this kingdom in the making of looking-glass plates." But mirrors did not become common until after the Restoration, when the Duke of Buckingham set up his celebrated works at Vauxhall. They were expensive luxuries, however, and even in the middle of the eighteenth century were the most costly items in bills of furnishing.

The term "cabinet" is often loosely applied to furniture of various kinds, but in strict language the cabinet is a box-shaped structure fitted with small drawers. It may have been introduced into Europe from the East, possibly by way of Venice or through the Moors in Spain. Small painted cabinets were made in England in the early part of the seventeenth century, but it was not till the time of Charles II. that the cabinet became an important piece of furniture. At that date cabinets are found mounted on stands and often decorated with lacquer or marquetry. At a time when insurance companies did not exist it was common to fit cabinets with secret compartments for the disposal of valuables, but it seems unlikely that intelligent thieves would have been deceived by such primitive devices. The cabinet of this type went out of fashion by the second half of the eighteenth century, but the idea survived in the elaborate fittings of writing-tables, washstands, and dressing-tables.

CHAPTER IV

THE ROMANCE OF THE BEDSTEAD

ALL through the course of history, from the earliest times to modern days, the bedstead has been regarded with a kind of sentimental reverence. With it are associated the three most pregnant events in the life of a human being, the three great scenes in the human drama, first birth, then marriage, and lastly death. In the scenic setting of the romances, comedies, and scandals which for centuries have enlivened the tedium of a harassed world, the bedstead has usually held a commanding position. The Gods of Love and Sleep can equally claim it as their own.

Far back in the Middle Ages when the furniture even of noblemen's houses was of the simplest character, the bedstead was an important and decorative object. In illuminated manuscripts of the fourteenth and fifteenth centuries it is common enough to find representations of beds with testers, curtains and coverlets of vivid colours, often richly embroidered, sometimes in gold or silver, with diaper patterns or with heraldic and fantastical compositions. Inventories of the period give further details of the materials in common use. All kinds of woven and embroidered stuffs were found, velvets, silks and satins of brilliant blue or scarlet and sometimes of cloth of gold. The barbaric splendour of these upholstered beds was not altogether a matter of sentiment, for they were well supplied with pillows, blankets, sheets and mattresses, while the heavy curtains protected the sleeper from the cold. Moreover, for many centuries the bed-chamber was the only room where privacy could be obtained and where intimate scenes of social life could be acted.

The testers, curtains, and coverlets of these early beds completely covered the wooden framework, which was of the roughest and crudest character. For this an obvious reason existed. England was torn with civil war, and it was necessary for the families who occupied the castles and fortified dwelling-houses to be ready to move their possessions at the shortest notice. Therefore, anything in the nature of solid wooden structures was avoided. The chest was the commonest type of furniture, and in the chest the sumptuous bed-hangings, with other valuables, could be packed. The wooden framework of the bed, like the trestle table, was valueless, and could be taken to pieces or broken up.

By the time of the Tudors, however, when conditions were becoming more settled, furniture assumed a more solid and permanent character. In the reign of Henry VIII., bedsteads were made with panelled oak backs carved with linenfold and other ornament, and had slender wooden posts often adorned with geometrical ornament, lozenges, roses, and heraldic chargoo. Curtains, testers, and coverlets of various materials were still retained. As time went on the wooden framework became more and more important. By the time of Elizabeth it had taken a particularly solid and characteristic form. Posts, back, and tester by this time were made of solid wood, usually oak, but in the more extravagant cases of walnut. The posts had in the middle heavy bulbous ornaments (like a cup and cover), a peculiar device, the origin of which is problematical, though it may have been a fashion imported from Flanders. As a rule, the backs were carved in high relief with round arches containing floral ornament and separated by grotesques or terminal figures. Often a sense of colour was obtained by inlaying the ornament in light woods like holly or apple. Occasionally, though rarely, the whole surface was painted in colours. At Burderop Park in Wiltshire,

General T. P. Calley has an Elizabethan bed with typical characteristics but brilliantly painted on all the surface with red, yellow, and other primary colours.

There is an historic Elizabethan bed, the Great Bed of Ware, which for centuries has stood out as an object of curiosity and jest. On account of its abnormal proportions (measuring some 12 feet square) this specimen of English furniture has all through its history been regarded as something of a mystery, for no similar monstrosity seems to have been discovered either at home or abroad. Apart from its size, the Great Bed of Ware does not differ essentially from other examples of the Elizabethan period. Fashioned in oak, having foot posts with bulbous ornaments resting on an open base with columns, inlaid panels within arches on the head and carved terminal figures, it can be classified in design and decoration with typical bedsteads still found in country houses throughout the land. As far as historical evidence goes, it stood probably throughout most of its history in the Saracen's Head at Ware, until its removal to the Rye House, where it can now be seen by the public.

An unbroken chain of evidence exists to show that since the time of Elizabeth the Great Bed of Ware has been celebrated as an object of wonder and discussion. Not many years after it was first set up it received a lasting advertisement from Shakespeare, who in *Twelfth Night* had occasion to refer to it :

" *Sir Toby Belch:* Go, write it with a martial hand; be curst and brief; it is no matter how witty, so it be eloquent and full of invention; taunt him with the licence of ink, if thou thou'st him some thrice it shall not be amiss; and as many lies as will lie in, thy sheet of paper, altho' the sheet were big enough for the Bed of Ware in England, set 'em down, go about it."

THE GREAT BED OF WARE.

About a hundred years passed before the bed seems again to have figured in historical literature. Sir Henry Chancy, in the *History and Antiquities of Hertford-shire,* published in 1700, makes a reference to it, and adds a humorous if somewhat gross story. Chancy relates that Ware was famous for its inns.

> " Wherefore one is very remarkable for a large Bed which is twelve foot square, the Strangeness of this unusual size oftentimes invited the curious Traveller to view the same; among whom 'tis reported that six citizens and their wives came from London in a Frolick to sport themselves; and when they had feasted their Bodies with the Rarities of the Town, the Women agreed that they and their Husbands would lie together in the great Bed, which was made ready for them."

Details of arrangement of husbands and wives were agreed upon, " but the Waggish Host discovering by the ill Management of their Bravery, and the Mode of their Speech, that they were not the persons they would be reputed, resolved to put a Joke upon them, the jest causing them to cut short their visit and return to London.

There was no particular change in the character of English bedsteads until the time of Charles II., when there occurred something like a revolution in social life. State bedsteads, after the Restoration and up to the time of Queen Anne, were usually of great height, with carved tester and head covered with the same materials as the curtains, often crimson, blue, or yellow damask or velvet bordered with fringes. A distinguishing characteristic was the bunches of feathers often found at the four corners of the tester. The origin of this decorative feature is obscure, though it may have been borrowed from the plumes associated with funeral hearses. English beds of this type bear a striking resemblance to the engraved designs of Daniel

Marot, a brilliant Huguenot artist, who emigrated from France to Holland after the Revocation of the Edict of Nantes and took service under William of Orange.

The desire for magnificent display at this period was fanned into flame by the extravagance of the King's mistresses. It is not to be wondered that Louise de Kerouaille, who claimed to be descended from half the best families in France, should have shown enterprise, judgment, and taste in furnishing and decoration. But it is a matter of some surprise that her English competitor, Nell Gwyn, who rose, as it were, from the pavement to a seat on the left hand of the throne, should have exhibited tastes in this direction. Evidence exists, however, to show that the ex-orange girl of Drury Lane was ambitious to keep pace with her patrician rival as a connoisseur in the arts. The staircase of Nell Gwyn's house at Windsor was painted by the famous artist Verrio, and among her papers which have been preserved are various bills for furnishing of considerable interest. The most remarkable items in these accounts refer to a silver bedstead, which must have been an object of unusually fantastic originality. The document is headed:

"*Work done for ye righte Honble. Madame Guinne. John Coquus silversymyth, his bill,*"

and consists of some forty items, of which the total cost was £1,135 3s. 1d. From the various entries it is possible to form some conception of this remarkable bedstead. It had a wooden framework with a "greatte bord for ye head of ye bedstead and for ye other bord that come under it."

The whole seems to have been covered with plates of silver and adorned with numbers of ornamental devices. Among the latter were silver models of the King's head, figures of slaves, eagles, and cupids, and —strangest of all—a representation of Jacob Hall dancing on a tight rope of wire. Jacob Hall, famous at the time as an acrobat, was numbered among the Countess of Castlemaine's miscellaneous collection of lovers.

There is little doubt that Nell Gwyn was stimulated in her decorative ambitions by her rivalry with Louise de Kerouaille. Whatever the Frenchwoman did, Nell Gwyn was prepared to go one better—or worse. An authenticated portrait of Louise comparatively undressed was followed by one of her rival, described as "Madam Gwyn's picture, naked, with a Cupid by Lely," the painting being concealed by a shutter, and described in the catalogue of James II.'s pictures. Pennant, who wrote a history of London at the end of the eighteenth century, stated that in Nell Gwyn's house in Pall-Mall there was, within the memory of his contemporaries, a room of which all the walls and ceilings were covered with mirrors. The taste for "cabinet de glaces" was much favoured by fashionable prostitutes in Venice, Paris, and elsewhere at this period and during the eighteenth century. Louise de Kerouaille is reputed to have put up one of these rooms in her apartments, and no doubt helped to introduce the fashion into England, although the expense must have been very great on account of the rarity of glass. If Nell Gwyn placed the silver bedstead in her chamber of mirrors, the effect must have been dazzling, and we must give her full marks for audacity.

All through the eighteenth century the bedstead continued to hold a position of importance in the furnishing of the house, and much attention was often devoted to its decoration. Although still formed of a tester supported on posts, with hangings of various materials, it assumed more normal proportions than had been the fashion in the late Stuart period. By the middle of the eighteenth century, when the art of wood-carving had reached its zenith, the wooden structure of the bed became more important. Posts of walnut or mahogany were often delicately carved, and testers were boldly shaped in the rococo style. Sometimes the design took the form of a pagoda with lattice work, all the surface lacquered and gilt in the Chinese style. Chippendale gave many designs for bedsteads in the *Director,* and among more normal examples, illustrated a fantastic composition with allegorical figures, to which he gave the following description:

> " A Design of a State-Bed which I submit to the Judicious and Candid for their Approbation. There are found Magnificence, Proportion, and Harmony. If the Pedestals of the Bedstead, the Pillars, Cornice and Top of the Dome, are gilt with burnished Gold, and the Furniture is suitable, the whole will look extremely grand, and be fit for the most stately apartment. The ingenious Artist may also, in the Execution give full scope to his Capacity. The Bedstead should be six or seven Feet broad, seven or eight Feet long, and the whole Height fourteen or fifteen Feet. A Workman of Genius will easily comprehend the Design. But I would advise him, in order to prevent Mistakes, to make first a Model of the same at large; which will save both Time and Expense."

If the drawing had been worked out we can quite imagine that it would have looked "extremely grand," and even if a workman of sufficient genius to comprehend the design had been discovered, it is unlikely that he would have possessed a sufficient amount of courage to attempt the execution of the model.

At Osterley Park in Middlesex there is a bedstead of particular splendour, which might be considered as the last historic bedstead which England has produced. It was designed by Robert Adam, who made a detailed drawing for it, now preserved in the Soane Museum.

In form it consists of a dome with cornice, supported on inlaid posts with gilt metal capitals and bases, the cornice surmounted by winged sphinxes and the dome carved and gilt. Valances of pale green velvet embroidered with characteristic ornament hang in festoons beneath the cornice, while curtains and coverlet all designed in unison complete the composition.

The Napoleonic wars produced a period of depression, when the popular cry was economy and the arts languished through neglect. Nevertheless, imposing bedsteads in the Empire style with gilt eagles and purple hangings were sometimes made for great houses. But the period of history was passing, never to return, when the bedstead could be regarded as an object fraught with romance and human interest. Victorian sensibility wrapped the bedroom in a strict privacy unknown to earlier and more natural times; and modern hygiene has condemned as insanitary the rich hangings which once gave colour to the scene and comfort to the sleeper.

CHAPTER V

THE STORY OF CHIPPENDALE

THOMAS CHIPPENDALE in his own day was evidently a man of considerable vanity, but if his shade could return to earth we are inclined to think he would be dazzled and perhaps slightly puzzled at the immense and apparently permanent notoriety which his personality has attained throughout the civilized world. What is the reason that public opinion has elected to place a single English cabinet-maker on a pedestal of fame and adopt his name as a household word? Why is it that for a generation or more, without historical inquiry, the term " Chippendale " has been chosen to express a certain period or style of English furniture? It is not a case in which public opinion can flatter itself on an instinctive ability for recognizing talent, for until recent years nothing was actually known of Chippendale's workmanship or his merits as a craftsman. It might be described as a case in which public opinion backed a winning horse, but in the dark.

There is little doubt that Chippendale's fame originally owed its birth to his publication, *The Gentleman and Cabinet-maker's Director,* an imposing octavo volume first brought out in 1754, and containing 160 plates of designs for furniture, with an introduction and explanatory notes. Copies of this book are now comparatively rare, but all through the nineteenth century the book was known to specialists, furniture-makers, and collectors, and to a certain extent to the general public. No knowledge of English furniture existed, and the book served as a useful key to the elements of the subject as far as the eighteenth century was concerned. Consequently the term " Chippen-

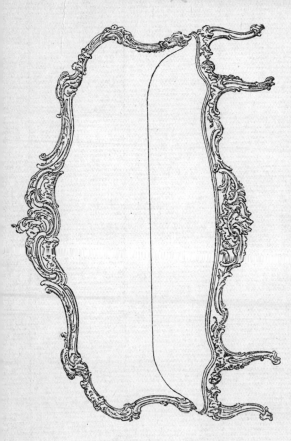

SOFA.   FROM AN ORIGINAL DRAWING BY CHIPPENDALE, 1754.

dale " was adopted by dealers and others as an explanatory label for a vast amount of mahogany furniture of the eighteenth century, and the public made use of the expression without bothering much about its meaning.

Chippendale therefore came to be recognized as a person of some national importance, and in the second half of the nineteenth century short biographies in dictionaries, founded more on imagination than fact, came to be written about him. It is immaterial who first started the legend, but some biographer of standing stated with no apparent authority that there were two Thomas Chippendales, father and son, who came from Worcester and set up business in London. This tradition persisted for many years. The first really important discovery was made some twenty or more years ago by the late Mr. Percy Macquoid, who found in two Yorkshire country houses, Nostell Priory and Harewood House, most elaborate bills for furnishing by Chippendale's firm, and was able to identify many of the actual pieces of furniture mentioned. It is true that these bills were rather later in date than the *Director,* and the furniture bore no resemblance to Chippendale's published designs, but this discovery made it possible to form an estimate of Chippendale's talents as a craftsman. About the same time the date of his death was established and many interesting facts about his private life and business were brought to light from authenticated records. Other important bills—those for furnishing David Garrick's house in the Adelphi and Mersham Hatch in Kent—were discovered at subsequent dates, and finally evidence was produced to show without doubt that the famous Thomas Chippendale was a native of Yorkshire.

Let us briefly sketch his career from the facts which are now in our possession. Born in 1727 at Otley in Yorkshire, he was the son of a village joiner, who was employed, according to tradition, on the Harewood estates, belonging to the Lascelles family. The young Thomas probably worked with his father, but, displaying unusual talent, was evidently sent up to London to learn the fine art of cabinet work. We know nothing for certain about this part of his career, but in 1748, at the age of about thirty, he married Catherine Redshaw at St. George's Chapel, Hyde Park.

He was evidently established in London at this date, for the poor rates books of St. Martin's show that he was living first in Conduit Court, Long Acre, and afterwards in Spur Alley Ward in the years preceding 1753, when he moved to St. Martin's Lane, which became the headquarters of his business during the rest of his life. Here he had a shop, offices, workshops, and a timber yard, his business increasing so rapidly that two years later he was renting three houses. In 1754 the first edition of *The Gentleman and Cabinet-maker's Director* was published from St. Martin's Lane. A slight set-back was experienced in the following year when a fire broke out in one of his workshops and destroyed the chests of twenty-two workmen. Chippendale at this time had a partner named James Rannie. Rannie died, however, in 1766, on which occasion a sale took place on the premises and all the stock was sold, consisting of a great variety of pieces of furniture as well as timber. The business was afterwards carried on at first in the name of Thomas Chippendale, but at a later date was known as Chippendale and Haig.

It is a matter of some surprise that, although in the eighteenth century great interest was taken in building and furnishing, no references have been found to Chippendale in contemporary letters or diaries. Yet he must have been a considerable celebrity in his own day. The list of subscribers to his book includes many names celebrated in public and social life as well as long lists of cabinet-makers who supported him by

RIBBON-CHAIR. CHIPPENDALE, 1754.

their subscriptions. Moreover, the records of his work for famous families showed that he must have enjoyed a great reputation among his contemporaries. He was proposed for the Society of Arts by Sir Thomas Robinson of Rokeby, and his signature is found in the old signature book of the Society on the same page with those of Horace Walpole, Robert Adam, Cipriani, Lord Pembroke, and other personalities well known in intellectual and fashionable society. Some of his business correspondence with Sir Edward Knatchbull of Mersham Hatch has been preserved, and from it we can judge that he was a fairly sharp man of business and that, prosperous as his affairs appeared to be, he was constantly hampered by lack of ready money. Although he executed numerous commissions both in the decoration and furnishing of country houses, there are good reasons for thinking that he often found it difficult to get his money. In this connection he figured as the principal creditor in a lawsuit brought in the Court of Bankruptcy in reference to the estate of the Italian adventuress Teresa Cornelys. This notorious personality, whose career is sketched in the celebrated *Memoirs* of Casanova, was well known in London on account of the entertainments which she gave professionally at her house in Soho Square. In order to dazzle the public she furnished the house with great extravagance, and for this purpose evidently employed the firm of Chippendale, the most fashionable decorators of the day. This happened six years before Chippendale's death, for he died of consumption in 1779, and was buried in the churchyard of St. Martin's-in-the-Fields. Two years previously he was married for the second time to Elizabeth Davis at Fulham Parish Church. He left a large family, of which the eldest son, Thomas, carried on the business for many years.

We have suggested that the origin of Chippendale's fame, as far as the public is concerned, can be traced to his famous publication *The Gentleman and Cabinet-maker's Director*. This most ambitious work is an important document in the study of the domestic history of England in the eighteenth century. Its engraved plates include types of furniture of all kinds, extravagant examples such as were made for great mansions, and simpler pieces suitable for the middle classes. In making the designs Chippendale borrowed from all sources that came to hand. He was greatly influenced by the French rococo style, being familiar with it through the designs of Meissonier, though he also experimented with the Chinese and Gothic fashions when public taste was leaning in such directions. Plagiarist as he may have been, he succeeded in evolving a style which was both individual and characteristic. The preface to the book gives the impression that he was a jealous and egotistical man. His descriptive notes to the plates mark him as a thoroughly conscientious workman who devoted immense attention to the technical details of his craft. The notes show, also, that, contrary to the popular idea, he had no particular leaning to mahogany as a medium of expression, but that a large proportion of his models were intended to be finished with gilding or lacquer. The *Director* was evidently a great success at first, for a second edition was published in the following year, but a third and enlarged edition brought out in 1762 probably fell flat, as the models depicted were by that time going out of fashion.

Chippendale was evidently a man who, to use a modern expression, was always "right up to the minute," and one who had no use for lost causes or unsuccessful enterprises. It is therefore quite natural to find him associated towards 1770 with Robert Adam in the new school of Roman and Etruscan decoration which was supplanting the rococo style and the absurd Chinese and Gothic fashions. We find him working with the Adam brothers during the last ten years of his life, and consequently turning his back on the type of work which he had introduced to the public in the plates of the *Director*. From the evidence of accounts we know that his firm was employed to execute both furniture and decoration in various houses in which Adam acted as architect—Nostell Priory and Harewood House in Yorkshire, as well as Mersham Hatch in Kent and David Garrick's house in Adelphi Terrace. Though Robert Adam designed both the furniture and decoration of the houses which he was engaged on building or restoring, it required the technical knowledge of the cabinet-maker to work out the designs, and it is not surprising to find Chippendale's firm was employed on important occasions to carry out this work. In these transactions there are no records of the personal relations existing between Adam and Chippendale. All honour must be paid to Robert Adam, whose intellectual force and classical knowledge contributed so largely to form the style associated with English decoration and furniture in the latter part of the eighteenth century. On the other hand, every credit must be given to Chippendale, whose technical skill was able to translate into reality the complicated, difficult, and highly ornamental designs which were set before him. Much of Chippendale's authentic work at Harewood and Nostell, whether carved, gilded, inlaid, or lacquered, stands out among the world's masterpieces in this branch of human achievement.

We have endeavoured to show that Chippendale can be regarded from two distinct aspects. He has for years been looked at as a shadowy personality who published a famous book of designs for furniture to which the popular conception of the Chippendale style owed its origin. This did not prove him to be a practical cabinet-maker of any importance, but it happens that the discovery of bills making it possible to identify his finished work has latterly proved him to be a craftsman of supreme excellence. He is therefore worthy of a place in history both as the author of the most ambitious work of its type ever produced and as the most brilliant practical cabinet-maker which England can lay claim to.

CHAPTER VI

THE VICTORIAN PERIOD—AND AFTER

In reviewing the arts of a country, whether architecture, painting, sculpture, decoration, or furniture, it is a difficult matter to decide at what period progress of development was definitely arrested and a state of decadence had begun to set in. At what time in English history have the decorative arts arrived at their highest pitch of excellence? The Elizabethan and early Stuart age, vigorous and simple, with panelled rooms and oak furniture designed in unison, though admirable in every respect, reflected a comparatively primitive civilization. Historically this age is crowded with romance, but its furniture has largely an antiquarian interest, and cannot be considered suitable to the more complex and subtle tastes of the present day. The graceful walnut furniture which became fashionable after the Restoration showed a great advance both in artistic sensibility and in general usefulness, corresponding with a refinement in manners partly due to foreign influence. By the middle of the eighteenth century, when the personality of Chippendale predominated, still greater progress is noticed. The simpler furniture of this school, with its admirable proportions, shapely mouldings, and excellent joinery, all systematically studied, leaves nothing to be desired, and presents models which could probably not be improved upon. Even on the Continent English furniture of this date was highly esteemed by contemporary judgment. Nor did the latter years of the eighteenth century show any falling off in general excellence. The style usually associated with the name of Sheraton (a theoretical

designer much more than a practical cabinet-maker)
when satinwood was in high favour, is distinguished
for purity of line and skilful arrangement of ornament
in inlay or painting. Moreover, it was essentially
practical, and went further in elaboration of fittings
than any of the styles which had gone before.

Although individual taste may favour the work of
one period rather than another, it may be said that
up to about the year 1800 a gradual development towards an improved order of things can be traced, combined with a more and more intelligent conception of
the proper functions of furniture. But from the beginning of the nineteenth century onwards the subject
seems to have been robbed of all policy and idealism
and to have degenerated into a confused jumble of
trivial and misguided notions. It must be admitted
that the time of the Napoleonic wars was not favour-
able to artistic achievement, though the age produced a
few great figures in imaginative literature. But the
borrowed Empire style and the rather pathetic experi-
ments in Greek and Egyptian design carried neither
conviction nor satisfaction. The cabinet-makers of the
eighteenth century had a bold and progressive policy,
but their descendants in the nineteenth century seem
to have been mainly engaged on the hopeless task of
chasing shadows.

Although the Victorian age brought a return to
national prosperity, it witnessed some astounding per-
formances in the matter of public taste. The peculiarly
stuffy and depressing rooms of the mid-nineteenth
century, with their confusion of trivial furniture, are
regarded at this distance of time with a certain tolerant
amusement. Parodies of every style, from the Middle
Ages onwards, were found side by side with novelties
like *papier mâché* articles of every description and
ornaments of shells and wax flowers. Actual workmanship in furniture was usually sound, but the
designers of the day seem to have had no appreciation

of line, form, colour, nor decorative arrangement. No attempt was made to treat a room as a complete composition, as had been the case up to the end of the eighteenth century. In Robert Adam's interiors every piece of furniture was designed to occupy a definite place in the architectural scheme, and even in middle-class houses of the period there was usually found only a sufficient amount of furniture to satisfy the social needs of everyday life. In Zoffany's paintings of domestic scenes about 1770 and thereabouts there is a marked similarity in the furnished rooms forming the background to his family groups. Most sitting-rooms had a circular table with tripod base and possibly a card-table, screen, or spinet, with a sufficient number of chairs and couches to supply the needs of the family and guests; walls were papered or covered with damask, on which were probably fixed a pair of sconces and a few mirrors and pictures. A certain breadth and simplicity characterized the whole arrangement, forming a sharp contrast to the overcrowded and haphazard arrangement of the Victorian home. This result was intensified by the habit in the nineteenth century of collecting works of art of all types irrespective of uniformity or suitability. After the French Revolution, for instance, when the aristocracy of France were obliged to dispose of their inherited possessions, England had the opportunity, and made the most of it, of securing the masterpieces of painting, sculpture, furniture, and china which circumstance had thus put on the market. Henceforth, therefore, in the great houses of the country, Boulle wardrobes and writing-tables and the like were usually found striking an extra discordant note in an already unbalanced composition.

At the Great Exhibition of 1851 an attempt was made, with startling results, to show the people what could be done in the way of ambitious artistic achievement. The extraordinary amount of money, ability, and energy that was wasted in this movement purely

through misguided principles is summed up in Traill's
Social England without exaggeration :

> " In furniture, though we have since returned
> to the elegant but thin lines and the sparse sur-
> face decoration of the eighteenth-century de-
> signers, inspiration was sought, during the twenty
> years of triumphant vulgarity between 1840 and
> 1860, in the never-forgotten late Renaissance and
> French decadence; while a market was found also
> for the ' Wardour Street Gothic ' of the archi-
> tects of the new school. Some quite amazing
> drawing-room cabinets and consoles were evolved
> —decorations including star-spangled niches with
> statues unimpeachable in their decorous marble
> nakedness, patriotic groups of England's soldiers
> in cast bronze, gilded griffons, trophies of arms
> and cornucopias of peace and plenty. Ebony
> tables inlaid with silver were reserved for the
> wealthy, while paltry imitations of them satisfied
> the poorer classes. Beds were grandiose and
> superb—carved and polished, and hung with
> heavy curtains with valances round, sometimes
> embroidered with medallions emblematic of the
> domestic virtues in tent-stitch."

The inevitable reaction arrived. The cry of " Back
to Nature and the primitives " which Ruskin preached
and the Pre-Raphaelites practised went some way
towards nailing down the coffin of the exuberant vul-
garity of the mid-Victorian tradition. In the decorative arts the pendulum swung back to the vigorous
simplicity in design with the vivid colouring of the
Gothic period, and, unlike most Gothic revivals, found
its inspiration in the spirit of the time as much as in
the form. Unquestionably the personality of William
Morris, though limited in outlook and prejudiced,
went a long way towards the improvement in con-

temporary public taste. In the design and colouring of
textile fabrics and wall-papers and in printed pages
the influence of his teaching is still felt at the present
day. It is doubtful, however, whether his principles
had much effect in the matter of furniture. Neither
the furniture which Morris designed or made, nor that
of the Cotswold school which carried on his tradition,
seem to have made much impression on the public in
general. For this various reasons might be put
forward. It may be that it has never been sufficiently
advertised; it may be that it possessed an affectation
appealing only to a limited group or a certain
amateurishness and crudity which prevented it—as the
saying is—from carrying across the footlights. The
fact that its principles condemned machinery and
ruled that all cabinet-making should be worked by
hand tended to alienate it from the progressive tendencies of modern life.

There was another movement in the last quarter of
the nineteenth century which was beginning to have a
far greater influence on public opinion. This was the
revival in interest in the historic styles of English
furniture. At the time of the Great Exhibition a slight
attention had been paid to English furniture of the
eighteenth century, and elaborate models based on
Chippendale's designs were worked out in the solid.
But in a general sense ignorance of this subject was
profound. It was not till some thirty years ago that
enthusiasm and investigation on the part of individuals
and the photographing of examples throughout the
country brought a knowledge of English furniture
within the reach of the general public. Its undoubtedly
excellent qualities began for the first time to be
realized. Chairs, tables, cabinets, and the like, which
for many years had been condemned to the garrets,
were now brought back to favour and welcomed like
relatives returning from unjust banishment. This revival has had both good and bad effects. It has resulted

in the market being flooded with copies of English furniture of the sixteenth to eighteenth centuries, a movement for which some defence can be made, in spite of the gulf between modern life and past centuries; nothing, of course, need be said about forgeries imitating the effects of time with intent to deceive. It has left an indelible mark on the bulk of modern English furniture, which, consciously or unconsciously, finds inspiration in the shapes and ornaments designed by the cabinet-makers of the past. When this means appreciation of graceful form and line, good mouldings, and proportion and judicious arrangement of ornament, all intelligent critics will agree as to its desirability, especially when combined with suitability of purpose and recognition of modern needs.

There is, however, another school, the school of advanced modernity, which views all tradition with contempt. This attitude is found in all branches of modern art. The desire for novelty and change, however, is innate in human nature, and it is doubtful if there is anything new in this type of mentality. It has existed among small cults for centuries, and probably the oldest civilization had its advanced thinkers who imagined they had discovered new secrets of absolute originality. The apostles of this belief declare that it is as absurd to-day to use the furniture of the seventeenth or eighteenth centuries (or seek inspiration from it) as it would be to wear the clothes which were fashionable at those dates. This makes no allowance for the fact that clothes last only a few years and that a well-made chair, table, or chest of drawers can be used for centuries. It is also generally admitted by those who combine an average amount of sanity with good taste that much of the furniture of the seventeenth and eighteenth centuries agrees admirably with purely modern couches and chairs with their excellent upholstery, based, incidentally, on the figured stuffs of the past, both Eastern and Western. It is perfectly true that machinery and modern inventions make it possible to design new types of furniture essentially useful and suitable for the present generation. But it savours of perversity when it is considered clever to ignore all recognized rules of composition and to twist wood into unnatural shapes, through a mistaken conception of originality. In all these matters it is a case of what gives us the greatest pleasure to live with, and it is doubtful if many people would find satisfaction in furnished interiors resembling a background to the Russian Ballet.

BIBLIOGRAPHY

Bolton, A. T. : *The Architecture of Robert and James Adam.* (1922.)

Brackett, Oliver : *Thomas Chippendale.* (1924.)

Cescinsky, Herbert : *English Furniture of the Eighteenth Century.* (1909.)

Chippendale, Thomas : *The Gentleman and Cabinet-maker's Director.* (1754, 1755, 1762.)

Dictionary of English Furniture. By P. Macquoid and R. Edwards. 3 vols. (Country Life, 1927.)

Evelyn, John : *Diary.* Edited by H. Wheatley. (1906.)

Gotch, J. A. : *Growth of the English House.* (1909.)

Hepplewhite, A. : *Cabinet-maker's and Upholsterer's Guide.* (1788.)

Jourdain, M. : *English Decoration and Furniture.* (1923.)

Macquoid, Percy : *History of English Furniture.* (1904.)

Pepys, Samuel : *Diary.* Edited by H. Wheatley. (1893-1899.)

Shaw, Henry : *Specimens of Ancient Furniture.* (1837.)

Sheraton, Thomas : *The Cabinet-maker and Up-holsterer's Drawing Book* (1791); *The Cabinet Dictionary* (1803).

Smith, George : *The Cabinet-maker and Upholsterer's Guide.* (1826.)

Traill, H. D. : *Social England.* (1902.)

Victoria and Albert Museum : *Catalogues of English Furniture.* Vol. I. *Gothic and Early Tudor* (1923); Vol. III. *Late Stuart to Queen Anne* (1927).